Bidenomics: The Meanin
Policies to the American Dream and His
2024 Presidential Bid.

By

Gregory D. Richardson

Copyright

Table of Contents

Chapter 1: Bidenomics Explained - Why Biden's Policies Are Beneficial To Americans' Finances

President Joe Biden is attempting to increase public support for his initiatives to improve salaries and lower consumer prices as the 2024 presidential race heats up.

According to polls, Americans give Biden poor grades for his economic performance amid a two-year inflation rise that has subsided but is still historically high. According to a survey conducted by The Associated Press-NORC Center for Public Affairs Research last month, just 33% of respondents say they are satisfied with how he is managing the economy.

It will take time for Americans to see the benefits of new legislation, Biden said in a speech in Chicago on Wednesday. Biden was praising a collection of measures that the White House has started to refer to as "Bidenomics."

And I'm not here to announce economic triumph, said Biden. "I'm here to announce that we have a strategy that is drastically improving the situation. However, we still have work to do.

In general, according to Biden, his stimulus package quickly rescued the economy from the pandemic-caused downturn. However, many claim it went too far and contributed to the escalating inflation and increasing interest rates that put the United States on the verge of another recession.

What's Bidenomics?

The followings are Biden's primary assertions and an examination of his economic plan - "Bidenomics":

Quickest recovery and least inflation

According to Biden, his measures have resulted in the world's major economies experiencing the greatest recovery and the lowest inflation. In general, experts agree that this is true.

Give credit to the $1.9 trillion COVID-19 rescue program, the American Rescue Plan (ARP), which Biden led and which Congress approved in March 2021. It sent $1,400 stimulus cheques to the majority of families, extended substantial jobless benefits, and increased support for small companies, among other measures.

According to Mark Zandi, chief economist of Moody's Analytics, the rescue plan was necessary since the economy was in danger of entering a second recession after $4 trillion in similar COVID-19 relief measures in 2020.

"We didn't know how well the COVID vaccine was going to work," claims Zandi. Who could have predicted how the epidemic would develop? You should err on the side of doing too much if there is any doubt.

According to Zandi, 4 million fewer employment would have been produced in 2021 without the rescue plan.

Conservative economists counter that because the economy had already recovered from the COVID-19 recession, no boost was required. Just before Congress approved the bailout plan, employers had created more than 1 million jobs over the first two months of the year.

However, COVID-According to a senior economist at the libertarian Cato Institute Chris Edwards, the 19 vaccines were ramping up swiftly and many consumers were picking up other activities like eating out again. He contends that as a consequence, even without significant government assistance, the 22 million jobs that the health crisis destroyed were ready to return.

"It was overkill," says Edwards.

According to him, the outcome was a consumer spending boom that contributed to inflation reaching a 40-year high of 9.1% in June 2022.

Although many economists attribute price increases worldwide to supply chain bottlenecks caused by COVID-19, inflation in the United States was much greater than in Europe in 2021. According to Douglas Holtz-Eakin, head of the conservative think group American Action Forum, the discrepancy might be linked to the rescue plan.

Zandi claims that the plan's impact on inflation was only moderate. He claims that in the summer of 2021, COVID-19's delta variation exacerbated problems with Asian supply and increased consumer pricing. Supply chains were further hampered by Russia's conflict in Ukraine, which further increased inflation and commodity costs.

According to research company Trading Economics, U.S. inflation is now lower than the 6.1% inflation rate in the euro area, at 4%.

Jobs, but decent ones as well
The White House claims that Biden's policy has produced "good jobs" in addition to a record 13 million jobs in only two and a half years.

According to a White House study, employers are providing greater wages, better benefits, and more flexible schedules to recruit and keep employees.

The percentage of those aged 25 to 54 who are employed or searching for employment is at 83.4%, the highest level since 2007, the report stated.

Zandi concurred that the rescue package boosted consumer and business demand, driving firms to ramp up recruiting although many employees were taking early retirement or leaving the workforce due to COVID-19-related issues. As a result, there was a labor shortage, average annual earnings increased by 5%, and many people left their jobs in search of better-paying ones.

But according to Edwards, the lessening epidemic, not the stimulus, was mostly responsible for that hot job market. Additionally, he claims that the increased unemployment benefits included in the plan served as an incentive for employees to put off returning to the workforce even while job possibilities increased.

The middle class's growth
According to the White House, Biden's measures "helped put middle-class Americans in stronger financial position than they were in pre-pandemic." "Americans have higher net worth and higher disposable incomes (after inflation)"

According to Biden, wages for low-wage employees have increased at the quickest rate over the last 20 years.

According to Zandi, the strong increase in housing and stock values early in the crisis, together with savings from many stimulus payments, is the reason why Americans are richer than they were before COVID-19.

For a large portion of the epidemic, pay increases lagged below inflation, making it difficult for low- and middle-income people to keep up. However, inflation-adjusted disposable income, a more inclusive measure that also takes into account Social Security, investments, and other sources of income, is already outpacing its pre-crisis level.

Furthermore, Biden cites his extensive legislation to fund US infrastructure, increase US renewable energy output, and promote US chip manufacturing, all of which he claims would lead to the creation of quality middle-class employment.

Additionally, he points out that the Inflation Reduction Act benefits middle-class Americans by lowering the cost of prescription drugs and capping insulin pricing for seniors at $35 per month.

I believe that by investing in the nation's infrastructure and providing incentives for semiconductor manufacturers to increase production in the U.S., Vice President Biden's economic policies were successful in quickly returning the economy to full employment and will be beneficial in boosting its long-term competitiveness and productivity, according to Zandi.

But according to Edwards, the more than $2 trillion in investments would increase the

$32 trillion national debt and stifle competition by favoring certain companies over others. According to him, the increased expenditure would result in more taxes being paid by future generations.

Zandi concurs. He claims that the fact that Biden's budgetary policies have greatly increased the national debt burden is their "biggest failing."

Chapter 2: Biden Accepts "Bidenomics"

Less than two weeks after making a joke about "Bidenomics" in front of a crowd of union members, President Biden has finally stopped worrying and grown to enjoy it.

Why it matters
By completely aligning himself with a White House communications team that wants to run on the president's legislative and economic successes in 2024, Biden would fully embrace a term about which he has previously voiced some reluctance.

Top Biden aides have taken the calculated choice to own the economy, knowing that Republicans would attempt to pin the blame for a slowdown on them whether it is real or imagined.

Since the debt limit was lifted and Biden has no influence over the Fed's intentions to increase interest rates, the fight over the economy in the next 16 months will center on perceptions.

What they're saying

The president said at a speech on Wednesday in Chicago that "Bidenomics is working," and he's likely to receive the Democratic nomination there in a little over a year. "The middle class was let down by the trickle-down theory."

Driving the news

Biden argued with reporters over the meaning of the term "Bidenomics" to start a day that was meant to be devoted to embracing his economic accomplishments.

"You guys gave it a brand. Over the sound of Marine One's engines, he muttered, "I didn't. I never referred to it as Bidenomics.

"Let's be clear: The Wall Street Journal published it for the first time. OK? Continuing his defense of the word's derivation, Biden stated, "I don't go around shouting, 'Bidenomics,'"

When asked whether he dislikes the word, Biden said, "It's okay. Yes, that's okay since that's my policy.

By the time Biden spoke to a welcoming crowd at the iconic Post Office structure in the heart of Chicago, his support was more strident.

To cheers, he continued, "I'm pleased to call it Bidenomics.

The intriguing part is that on April 7, 2021, Greg Ip of The Wall Street Journal neutrally referred to it as "Bidenomics," saying that "while the successor to neoliberalism lacks a label, Bidenomics will do for now."

The White House, however, believes that the phrase entered the public lexicon via C-SPAN as a result of an insult said by Kevin McCarthy (R-Calif.), then-House Minority Leader, in May 2021.

Republicans are adamant about preventing the term's redefining, with McCarthy tweeting an image that is a copy of a White House graphic and declaring: "Bidenomics is about blind faith in government spending and regulations."

The overall picture
Two undeniable—and incongruous—facts concerning the American economy in 2023 are: Although the stats are astounding, Americans don't seem to be impressed.

The level of consumer confidence has risen to its highest point since early 2022. Durable goods new orders were up 1.7% last month, marking the third consecutive month of growth. According to the Labor Department's statistics for May, 339,000 jobs were created.

According to Neil Irwin of Axios, the so-called "misery index" – a combination of the jobless rate and inflation — has decreased dramatically over the last year.
On the other hand, a May AP-NORC survey found that just 1 in 4 Americans believe that the nation's economic situation is favorable.

The struggle for the economy in 2024 will mostly be a communication war in which both sides won't be averse to cherry-picking facts, as a result of these two dynamics.

Republicans will emphasize the persistently high inflation rate and a drop in real earnings. Additionally, GOP insiders will be prepared to seize any increase in unemployment or decline in growth.

On his leadership, 13 million jobs have been generated (and counting), and Biden will continue to tout massive investments in infrastructure and semiconductors.

Chapter 3: If 'Bidenomics' Works, Will It Be A Very Big Deal?

President Biden may not come off as a revolutionary, but he is overseeing a fundamental shift in the way the country views economics. He is not simply advocating a significant departure from Ronald Reagan's "trickle-down" policies, as Vice President Biden emphasized in a speech in Chicago on Wednesday. He is also rejecting many conventional wisdom that influenced the administrations of Democrats Bill Clinton and Barack Obama.

The government no longer hesitates to encourage investment in certain sectors and aims. Public works spending is back in vogue. The cornerstone of the country's foreign policy is no longer signing new free-trade agreements. Higher priorities include opposing monopolies and supporting unionization initiatives.

National security advisor Jake Sullivan made this argument in a significant speech of his own in April: "You can trace the break in part to new circumstances and challenges."

The article also includes the necessity of addressing climate change and the heightened competitiveness with China. The demise of many of the nation's industrial villages is also consistent with the long-term growth in wealth and income disparity. Resilience and domestic production were highlighted as a result of the pandemic's disruption of supply chains, particularly for semiconductors but also for other items.

The change is partly a result of who Biden is, his longstanding concern about the Democratic Party's alienation of people in the working and middle classes, and his dissatisfaction with the economic orthodoxy of the Reagan era that pervaded Democratic administrations.

He would regularly discuss his underlying unease with some of the dominant economic assumptions, particularly concerning trade and domestic investment, while I worked for him as vice president, Sullivan told me earlier this month.

The president now welcomes the term "Bidenomics," which he previously rejected due to its paternity for a school of economic thought. This shows how confident Biden and his lieutenants are in the current course. As he talked, the phrase was written on several posters within the Old Post Office.

Biden wants to demonstrate the effectiveness of his core ideas on infrastructure, climate change, and technology from a political standpoint. On Wednesday, he emphasized that they are creating well-paying employment for

Americans without college degrees and those who live in areas with "hollowed out" economies, who have suffered from the lack of economic progress.

The speech was a component of an organized administration-wide effort to combat economic uneasiness, which has resulted in Biden's lackluster popularity ratings despite historically high job growth. "A striking surge in construction spending for manufacturing facilities," which has doubled since the end of 2021, was lauded in a recent Treasury Department report.

Bidenomics has also spread internationally. A sign of this is the extraordinary and continuing discussion that Sullivan's speech sparked by advocating a "new consensus" to replace "a set of ideas that championed tax cutting and deregulation, privatization over public action, and trade liberalization as an end in itself." The outdated approaches, according to Sullivan, were ineffective on their own merits in addition to failing to address contemporary issues.

He said that "entire supply chains of strategic goods, along with the industries and jobs that made them, moved overseas" in the name of "oversimplified market efficiency." It was a promise made but not maintained that more trade "would help America export goods, not jobs and capacity." Specifically, he emphasized the need for "a modern American industrial strategy" and the advantages of "moving beyond traditional trade deals to innovative new international economic partnerships."

Sullivan assisted Hillary Clinton's 2016 campaign against Donald Trump, and the results of the election led to a long time of contemplation on the rage he saw throughout the nation.

In 2018, Sullivan stated in Democracy Journal, "I was reminded again and again how the broken aspects of the American economy were not the inevitable product of disembodied forces like 'globalization'; they were very much the product of policy choices shaped by decades of conditioning. As I traveled across the United States on behalf of the campaign."

The Biden-Sullivan initiative is essentially a deconditioning program. According to Sullivan, his speech "is a description not just of my journey on these issues" but also the path of his generation in response to "the shortcomings of the previous approach."

Can Bidenomics serve as the center-left's equivalent of Reaganomics' role as the center-right's model in the 1980s?

Anthony Albanese, the prime minister of Australia, and Keir Starmer, the head of the British Labour Party, have already echoed some of Biden's climate ideas in their approaches. The leader of the Australian Labor Party and former treasurer of the nation, Wayne Swan, told me that he thought Sullivan's speech was the finest economic talk in a decade. When describing her own "Securonomics," which has ties to Bidenomics, during a May visit to Washington, Rachel Reeves, a potential chancellor of the exchequer in Starmer's shadow government, cited it.

However, Biden is pushing his initiative aggressively because he is aware that its first test will be political. Only after Reagan's reelection was the reputation of Reaganomics assured. The same will apply to the phrase Biden first rejected but now holds in high regard.

Printed in Great Britain
by Amazon

42907435R00020